Reading Music
New and Selected Poems
By
Gary E. McCormick

Cover Layout and Design
by Jon Christopher McCormick
Cover Photography
by Mark Preston
Illustrations
by Jon Christopher McCormick and Perry Taylor

Published by GEM Press
Inquiries:
Gary E. McCormick
424 W. Ferry
Berrien Springs, MI 49103
jgmc4240@comcast.net

ISBN 0-9630037-2-0
Copyright, January 2011 by Gary E. McCormick

Acknowledgments

The Author gratefully acknowledges
the writers and editors of Peninsula Poets,
Mobius: The Poetry Magazine,
The Journal Era and The Herald Palladium
in which some of these poems
or versions of them first appeared.
Also, thanks to the songwriters, singers and musicians
whose music and lyrics inspired many of these poems.

Other poetry books by Gary E. McCormick
One of the Many Roses
Between Seasons

First to Jean
Whose spirit lingers
Mingles with my muse
Touching each word
With their spirits

And to the
Maker Of Music
Inspiring the Awe

And to all the
Music makers
Still bringing joy
By making music
Day by day
Day after day

One note at a time

Contents

1. Reading Music
2. Why There Will Never Be Silence
3. Bill Evans
4. Clooney
5. Dad Changes Tunes
6. Dave McKenna
7. Big Band Blast
8. Four Voices
9. Gonna Bounce The Moon
    Just Like A Toy Balloon
10. I've Heard Those Songs Before
11. Sims, Cohn, Getz Among Others
12. Jazz Piano
13. Salt Peanuts, Salt Peanuts
14. Six Feet Down Blues
15. Song Sparrow
16. The Blues Ain't Nothin'
    But A Pain In The Heart
17. I Say Tomayto, You Say Tomahto
18. Tremor
19. Waiting For Monty
20. Wind Chimes
21. Harold Who?
22. Celebrating A Long Time Of Love
23. The Great Love Story
24. Every Which Way
25. The Stone Hunter
26. Folding Socks
27. It's An Order
28. May We Dare To Assume
29. Some Final Words For Jean

30. A Brand New Poem
31. A New Crossing
32. A Peaceful Recollection
       During The Thunder Of War
33. Acknowledgment
34. Automaton
35. Bittersweet
36. Dissolution, Then More Questions
37. Early Green
38. Making The Rounds
39. Morning Window
40. For They Know Not What They Do
41. Nothing But Bluebirds All Day Long
42. Oblivion
43. Our Inviolable Flag
44. Pink Ribbon
45. Sailing Over The Rim
46. Signs of Autumn
47. Silence
48. The Great American Novel
49. Thinking It Through
50. Time
51. Walking With Dog
52. Warming Warning
53. Winter Rain
54. Writing About Nothing In Particular
55. Another Day
56. Pentecost
57. Skyrockets
58. Morning Chorus

Reading Music

The piano man unravels a mystic language
Spots and dots riding on five horizontal lines
Bars mathematically dividing the melody

The keyboard hammers strike the strings
Move forward keeping the tune's time
Knowing where they're going, not looking back

Eyes dart back and forth keeping time
Ten fingers land exactly where they need to be
Individually, in concert, spirited, subdued

The pianist is dead on, follows the ups and downs
Of the sure-footed notes as the eighty-eights
Sing what must be sung, this time with a flourish

My soul flutters and staggers from the impact
Of those dancing spots and dots of sound
I see them, I hear them, I feel them, I hum them

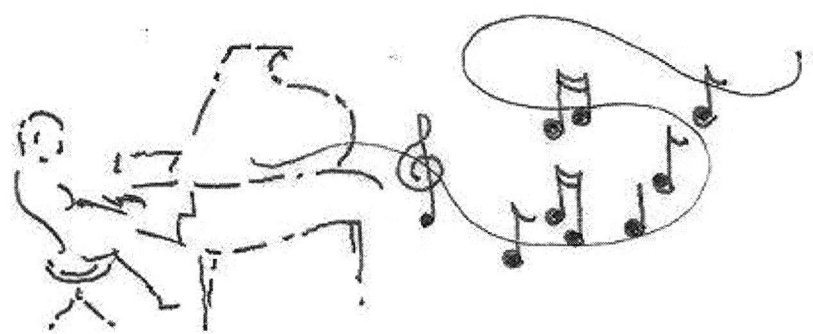

Why There Will Never Be Silence
              (*For Sarah Vaughn*)

When all is quiet
Not even a cricket screeching
My soul will still hear Sassy singing

Her velvet voice wraps around each word
Swirls them with her slow rolling vibrato
Tenderly stirs them into an evening breeze

Her scat solos play a horn
Trade razzmatazz with the snare
Touch the tapping feet of the crowd

If you haven't been to Birdland
She'll take you there with her lullaby
If you feel like a foggy day she'll make you shine

And I'm certain she will always break silence
And if they press the world's mute button
My mind's ear will always hear Sassy singing

Bill Evans

Melody architect:
Builder of pure piano lines
Assembling *Waltz for Debbie*

Lyrical trio:
Your favorite form
Dearly misses your precise chords

Distinctive music:
Brilliant improvisation
Building blocks of lyrical cathedrals

Your early finale:
Solos suddenly stopped
Player of addiction's last note

Now you're part of your *Peace Piece*

Clooney
  "Hey there, you with the stars in your eyes..."
                   Rosemary Clooney (1928-2002)

Today everything seems young on planet earth
Its springtime blossoms as colorful as a kaleidoscope
Wouldn't you know all is rosy-glow-well with the world
And blue-skies happy because I'm sitting on its top

I find myself, enjoying the youth of my seventies
Joyfully bawling my eyes dry as I reel and feel
Every heart-bouncing word as Rosie croons *Hey There*
Giving my soul a starry-eyed feeling of fifties nostalgia

My heart's a house and it's singing
Come on a my house, my house a come on

Dad Changes Tunes

You must have loved us dearly
Cared for us deeply, to trade your traps
For Ford's Rouge Steel payroll

Henry couldn't fathom your sacrifice:
You walking off the bandstand
Into the rusty open hearth dust
Quitting those snappy jazz solos
For its searing blast furnace heat

It must have burnt acutely
To trade your skins and cymbals
For the fire and dust of Ford

I think of this as I tap my foot to the
Basie beat of drummer Butch Miles

Dave McKenna

Can't bring your foot to tapping?
Let Dave's left hand get you going

The saloon player with the
Bouncing bass line
Stays true to the melody
As he improvises

Waiting for *C Jam Blues* to
To get you moving?
Let the southpaw
Start some rumbling thunder

Think there's a lull
In your dancing heartbeat?
Let Dave walk the dog
With a lefty's quick beat

Too, too quiet after
The right hands last riff?
Get some red-hot left-handed
Tempo going Dave's way

Do you find it hard
To mobilize your prancing feet?
Let the lefthander excite some
Booming rhythm in your bones

Those in the know
Call him a two-handed piano player
You can say that again
Praising his blazing bass line

Big Band Blast

The piano softly points the direction
Before the brass declare the pace
Set the screaming spirit of the flying
Hot swing of the fast jamming jazz band

Solos smoothly come and go, styling the mood
From sax to sax, trumpet to trumpet, bone to bone
Ivories wax eloquently to the beat
Of the snapping snare and breezy cymbals

Counterpoint blends of bass and eighty-eights
Bring on the fusion, then come to a cool conclusion

Four Voices

Crosby the crooner
Sings love songs solo
Duets with Frank, Ella, Rosie
To name just a few
Vocalizes on the road with Hope & Dot
Makes *True Love* to Grace
Inspires us as a singing priest

Sinatra makes the ladies swoon
Seduces the audience with blue eyes
Makes us bounce to big band rhythms
Riddle puts his label on the oldies

Torme scats a wordy drum solo
Turns the tempo down on a touching tune
Thrills souls with the magic of Kern, Gershwin,
Porter, Arlen, Berlin, Fields, Rogers, Mercer
Makes the best better as part of a rare medley

Bennet, crafts each work in Sharon's wake
Voice always puts a finger of the right key
Lets us know he loves every lyric, every melody
Puts his signature on another Hit Parade winner

Four voices, play gigs on stage, screen, tube, studio
Never miss a page as they sing the American songbook
Pay homage to composers, arrangers, lyricists, conductors
Joyfully take us for a ride with those soul filled melodies

Gonna Bounce The Moon
Just Like a Toy Balloon

We've heard those lyrics before

The crooners sing them
Explain their youthful playful hearts
Swing buoyantly at love's first bight

Hearts gulp at the top of a high flying swing
Gasp and pump as youth sings on the wing
Stretch out and up, touch, then helium-like, rise

Souls float and flutter like feathers together ascending

I've Heard Those Songs Before

Despite a childhood of uncertainty
Clouded by the Hiroshima of war
The lyrics and the music that sang them
Still stirs its medley, rousing youthful memory

Radio and records waxed the tunes
Indelibly in the grooves of my mind
Especially those big band classics

At that time I scanned the newspaper's columns
For killed in action, wounded and the missing
While hearing in the background Miller, Goodman
Dorsey brothers, Shaw, Basie and Ellington

I took a *Sentimental Journey* with Doris Day
Hummed Helen Forest's *Heard That Song Before*
While Artie Shaw took me *Dancing in the Dark*
Suffered through Elmo Tanner's *Heartaches*

Frightening war stories were always accompanied
By Barnet, Gray, Spivack and Kaye
*Begin the Beguine, Stardust, Tangerine
Amapola, Green Eyes, In the Mood,
I've Got My Love to Keep Me Warm*

If I want to turn loose a hornet's nest
Of sleeping forties' emotions, I let Martha Tilton's
And the Angels Sing do its thing

Sims, Cohn, Getz Among Others

Someone says
Music's beauty
Shows us the
Creator's face

So many times
You guys blew
Your cool sweet
Melodious sax solos

You improvise
Open hearts
Clear minds
Enchant souls

Always your smooth
Tarnished gold horns
Create crystal clear
Sharp-eyed views
Of that Shining Spirit

It's as close as I can get
To view the face of God

Jazz Piano

Both hands play
All eighty eight of 'em
Tickle tease tap out
Tempo rhythm melody
Syncopating dissonant
Soft slow pervasive
Symmetric sharp swirling
Ten fingers swing reckless
Loud clanging jamming
Percolating gliding brewing
Humming jumping jiving
Hammers out a wild riff
Bangs all black and white of 'em

Salt Peanuts, Salt Peanuts
   For John Birks "Dizzy" Gillespie

  "He was an extrovert player,
  His improvisations moved constantly outward
  And his solos tended to mirror him
  He often used a mute, and he ruminated"
         Whitney Balliett, The New Yorker

Dizzy muses
Dazzles with muted horn
Bell aslant sings brassy lyrics
Cheeks bloat, blows Steuben Glass solos

He ruminates
Chews some foot-tapping chords
Fingers flash a high-flying melody
Finishes with his *salt peanuts* signature

Six Feet Down Blues

They sway
Sing their deep down
Heartbreaking blues

Moaning and reeling
Weeping and wailing
Graveyard howls
For Satchmo's
Silent horn

How do you like
Those low down
Eulogy blues, Louie?

Song Sparrow

How do you put its whistle into words
Describe this bird whose song is sweetness pure?

I can only hint at its music as I sing sweetly with my pen
Send its sound flying from eye to ear, can you hear?

Look at its beauty as it broadcasts aloud
Does its song still trill through spring's dancing leaves?

Can you hear the wee bit of a thing
Voice its joy and spread it aloft?

Look up and listen as it
Makes high flying music, soaring on singing wings

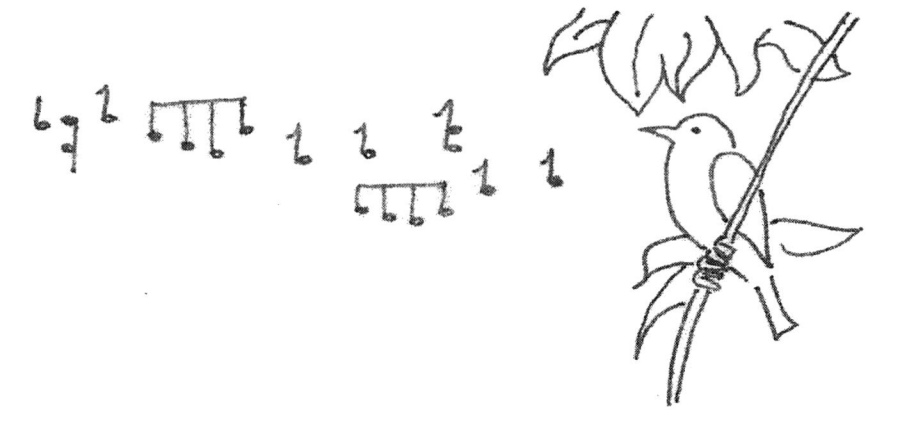

The Blues Ain't Nothin'
But a Pain in the Heart
          Billie Holiday

Anguish is what Lady cries
When she sings the blues
Wails her deep hurting heart

I hear her Holiday refrain
Swallow her bluesy pain
Wallow in its heartache

I weep while Billie sings
Those low down, I lost my lover
Deep blue, Lady Day blues

I Say Tomayto, You Say Tomahto

Ira Gershwin had a way
Of explaining a quandary
Choosing the right word or phrase
To clarify a stubborn conundrum
The kind when two people
Say things differently
But mean the same thing

Like those folks on both sides of the street
Holding signs expressing their certainties
One sign reads: Support The Troops, Send Them Ammo
The other: Support the Troops, Send Them Home

One wants to keep soldiers safe with more arms and armor
The other hopes to keep them safe and out of harm's way
Both sides of the street shout the strength of their convictions
They shake their signs and scream Potayto, Potahto,

The sign carriers are in no mood to agree to disagree
Ira Gershwin brings the singer's dilemma to an end
Concludes with these lyrics: *let's call the whole thing off*

Tremor
 "The tremor of awe is the best in man"
                    Goethe

The first three notes of this movement
Sends shock waves of vigorous awareness
Rising from the recesses of my soul

How can such beauty be recorded
By dancing dots and flags climbing
Up and down the score's fenced lines?

The conductor sways his baton
Waving through rhythmic space
Souls of music makers read and perform

The operatic overture makes every heart quiver
Rises gloriously to the very last demisemiquaver

Waiting for Monty

Monty Alexander vamps a long melodic improvisation
As bassist John Clayton and drummer Jeff Hamilton
Wait, with anticipating smiles, to leap in with their rhythm

The memories of the audience show silent grunts of mind
Attempting to put a finger on the chords whose combination
Will eventually give birth to a foot tapping, recognizable melody

Monty hits a chord, nods, and the trio sets off on their swinging
Rendition of *The Saints Go Marching In* without missing a beat
His fans know it's the last time they will ever hear this edition
Of the familiar and they show it with their standing ovation

Wind Chimes

I relax in a swinging hammock
Listening to those little pinging things
Ring and ting and they do a dazzle dance

I meditate on the overhead leaves
Wind flows over the silver of their underbellies
Swish and swoosh as they tremble and quake

I watch the tiptops of the trees
Swing and sway, lean and bend again
Still hear stuttering ding-a-lings of swinging chimes

Small wonder the wind also whistles its joyful tune

Harold Who?

"Who's Harold Arlen?"
Is what Truman Capote said
When asked to collaborate
On making a musical
Of one of his works

Well America's songbook
Begins with "A" as in
Arlen, Harold Arlen
Composer, songwriter, stylist

Sing a prayer was your ritual
Calling out melodies like
That Old Black Magic
Blues in the Night and *Get Happy*

Here's one thing you said:
Music doesn't argue, discuss or quarrel,
It breathes the air of freedom

The philosophy behind your magic music:
Don't waste your energy on the ugly,
Save it for the beautiful

You take Dorothy and your audience
From black and white to color and with Yip
Fly us *Somewhere Over the Rainbow*
The song that makes Gershwin bawl

Celebrating A Long Time of Love

Looking back over our fifty four years of marriage
Could make for a very long drawn out poem

I don't write long poems by choice
Trying to keep things short, sweet and simple

My love for you is not short
My love for you is not simple
Complex sweetness is our love

Our love is more than days, months or years long
Complicated by a half century
Of familial ups and downs, sadness and joy
Full of odds and ends of growls and calm

But thanks to our endurance
We more often than not have had
The most joyous times of our lives

And to think
It all began when our eyes met
On that one fine Michigan morning

The Great Love Story

Neither the one on the big screen
Nor the one between the novel's pages
For sure, not the one making today's headlines

Ours, the one that still makes our hearts ache
The one that began in September Fifty Five and endures
Surviving life's strains, stretch marks and strokes

It began with a long distance valentine
Grew six times in the maternity wards
Strongly continued through life's ins and outs

Often struggled with the day at a time stuff
Leveled during the times that count most
Still here today despite our memory's disability

It's our great love story, dear
Still being shared, still being written

Every Which Way

It comes at me
From out of the blue
Strikes me broadside
Sticks it to me harshly
Hits me where it hurts

My heart's beating pain
And the bite's a bitch
Wounds me every which way

Harder hearts were made
For sad nights like this

Grandma Jean McCormick by Grandson Perry Taylor

The Stone Hunter

Here comes that gray lady again
In her fishing hat and tote bag
Hunched over as she scours
The sand for the best of us

Look who's behind her
Like pied piper mice
They search stone after stone
Like their grandmother

I wish I could move on
My own accord so she
Would hold me and glimpse
At what a great stone I am

A wash of surf sweeps in
Pushes me close to her sandal
She bends, picks me up
And gives me a jeweler's eyeball

She drops me in her bag
And I bounce around
Dancing with her other finds

She uses her finger to
Separate the tiniest circles
Then her eye true to form
Settles on the littlest of us all

She calls us *Indian beads*
Blesses us with her broad smile
Acknowledges our native history
Honors our age-old traditions

Her grandchildren will follow
Curious in her sandy footsteps

Folding Socks

He aligns the matching pair
Smoothes them then tucks them
One into the other making a tight soft ball
Ready to be laid to rest in the sock drawer

His wife is failing
Heart and mind each day diminished
Recognition of the familiar
And of loved ones slipping away

Any thought of her illness
Is always accompanied by memories
Of the good days, the loving times

He bears this heartache
Joy and sorrow combined
Like the socks folded one into the other

It is sadness dark and intense
Mixed with bliss, exhilarating and joyful
It is a tight ball of joy-pain, explosive and extreme
Compressed into the folds of his wounded heart

It's An Order

Don't die on me now, dear
I'm not ready to drown in sorrow
I plan on you being here tomorrow

So don't leave me yet
I'm not looking forward to grief
To be alone without you is beyond belief

I insist you continue breathing
Extend your exit from this planet
Many others and me mean business dammit

So don't get anxious to leave this earth
Stick around a little longer to make life grand
Your appearance in tomorrow's obituary is banned

Get the picture? Don't depart!
Take a deep breath and make a fresh start
Stay another day and broadcast the beat of your heart

I demand that you stay around, don't leave now
So pay attention, it's an order, a direct order

May We Dare To Presume?

May we dare to presume
After all these years
That we have learned
Your grand design?

We often wondered:
What's the plan?

When I needed saving
Jean was sent to the rescue
So I could care for her
When she needed nursing

Not a bad plan for two
Grateful ageing lovers

Some Final Words For Jean

In so many words
I tell her it's okay to go
She has our permission

The hospice nurse
Calms my frantic call
Gives me instructions for the end

I put two drops on the spoon
Then under her tongue
It makes it easier to breathe
Quiets her rattle of death

I bring her ice for fever
She takes her last breath
And her lovely spirit vanishes
Leaves my lonely heart, sorrowful soul

I lost the love of my life
But I know exactly where she is
Dancing with celebrating angels
Laughing and spinning in His light

A Brand New Poem

Fresh from the wrapper
Just clipped from the umbilical
Thoughts as pink as a baby's bottom
Dressed in their newly sewn language

So let's have a look at you
Rearrange a few odds and ends
Change what comes first and last
Make sure the middle is as fit as a fiddle

Bit of advice
Beware of the critics
They'll try to psychoanalyze
Figure out what you're all about
Find out what you mean by that

So you better hide deep in a puzzle of riddles
Get lost in the fizzle and sparkle of razzle-dazzle
Let them label you cryptic, static and enigmatic

So be sure to make it short and sweet
And most of all keep it simple

A New Crossing
 (Read by the author at the dedication of the new bridge,
  Berrien Springs, Michigan, May 15, 1995)

It begins
We make our daily crossings
Then it ends, only to begin again

They waded across:
Our natives, our pioneers
Those who came before us
Who still make connections through history

The river St. Joe lifted their canoes
Bore their barges and fishing vessels
Carried the gaiety of their tour boats
Felt the strong gales for their sails
Smelled the smoke of their steamers

Then the builders crossed the stream
Erecting those bridges of the past
Wooden structures worthy of weight
Timbers touched by the erosion of time
Taken for granted, then taken away

Now this new concrete marvel
Arrives with the blossoms
Reminds us that bridges
Not only bear us up, but connect us
Force us to turn from the past
To cross with confidence into the future

A Peaceful Recollection
During the Thunder of War

Hardly a ripple moved the boat
As we fished for perch
On a quiet Michigan lake

My father and uncle
Helped bait my hook
And pulled up from the deep
Chilled jumbo bottles of beer

My bobber jiggled a first bite
When I heard the screams and
Firecracker explosions from shore
Then came the honking of horns
Wailing cry of sirens and the
Joyful ringing of bells and more bells

We looked toward shore
At my mother's flailing arms
As she called us home
To join the VJ Day celebration
On that joyous August afternoon

I think of this as I watch
Civilians react to the sirens
And sounds of deadly missiles
Honing in on their homeland

The news anchor tries to show
Some emotion as he reads
News copy of ghastly aerial carnage
Drones honing in on the middle east
Death squeezed onto the small screen

Acknowledgement

Thanks
For the thought
Your input of
Poetic inspiration

My gratitude to
Whomever It comes from
I like to call it a
Glorious inspiring spirit

My mind was asleep
Then suddenly you
Touched me with a spark

I wrote it down

Automaton

Touch it with those long pivoting arms
Lift and turn it upside down
Slide it sideways with precision
Place it exactly where it belongs

Time to take a break
Pause your boring actions
Put off repeating another
Senseless mechanical act

Let a poet insert a crowbar
Yank out the innards of your engine
Shake the sting from your nuts and bolts
Wrench panorama from your plunging pistons

Let me throw another switch
Push an awesome button

Bittersweet

It's a bittersweet morning sky
Blue with puffs of gray and white

My heart feels a chill of sadness
As I notice the vacated hummer feeder
Quiet for almost a week now

Then comes a jolt of joy when I spot
A returning junco dancing in scattered seed

Its excitement says snow will soon appear

Dissolution, Then More Questions

When that breath
I cannot catch is not caught
And the heaviness cannot be lifted

As the casket's plush softness
Cuddles my deep final sleep
Will answers greet my questions when I wake?

Eyes open, will my first sight
Be as colorful as all my autumns
Lyrics more poignant, melodies more uplifting?

Will fireworks dazzle the smiles
Of heaven's crowd of sparkling spirits?

Will an awesome voice trumpet:
"Dare we allow a poet loose in this simple place?"

That song will be music to my ears
And the spectacular view a sight for sore eyes.

Early Green

Careful little peek of green,
The sun may play its February trick
Forcing the teeth of morning's frost to nip you

Life's precarious
My faith says fight like the crocus
Persist, faint heart, push up to the light

It's a fight
Facing each day's fright
Praying for that early flower's might

Making The Rounds

There's lots of the
Same old same old going on
This tasty blue morning

As the redbib quickzips
Sticks its pollinated nose
Into the business of tiger lilies

First it sweeps in and kisses
The pumpkin orange buds
Of the sugar sweet flower

Then climbs to the drooping petals
Of the shady hosta hiding in shadows
Scoots to the butterfly bush's sweet scones

As an encore the hummer
Quickflys and dances updown
Darts back and forth for seconds
Then zips off on another flashflitting flight

Morning Window

The sun opens its blazing eyes
Slips its shine through the blinds
Wakes a houseplant sleeping in shade

A crystal hangs from a chain
Suspended from the windowsill
Changes the sun's colorful rays

The cat bats it with its paw
Sends its rainbows ricocheting
From wall to cabinet, floor to wall
Bounces its beauty about
Until it settles its swaying
Sends its color array
Scooting back into its prism

Then a single rainbow
Paints its multi-colored face
On the calico's shiny coat

Oh what a beautiful morning
Sings a passing song sparrow
Borrowing apropos Oklahoma lyrics

Its song wishes for more sunshine
To paint more early morning rainbows
With the window's swinging crystal

For They Know Not What They Do

He needed a fix
So he sold a lot of fixes
Didn't matter to whom
Wasted them to get wasted

She had one more for the road
Shots and beers not very feminine
The car staggering from side to side
Crashed and smashed against a tree

Speed is their drug of choice
The charge at the end of an accelerator
Squealing around the corner running
Head on into someone else's speed

Just one more random blast at anybody
Anger empties its shocking magazine
On every fear face ducking low
Shooter saves the last shots for his brain

Dead set on changing mankind's mind
Forcing them to think and do democratically
Dropping shock and awe from the heavens
Filling harm's way with the young and old

And so they go, on and on and on, ignorant
Doing more of the same old same old

Nothing But Bluebirds All Day Long

Here's something
To brighten our day:
We're still breathing

Probably ungratefully
Taking each breath for granted
As usual, hearts and souls blind

When smiles light our faces
We should be sure to thank
The Big Guy for that ear to ear
Look on our beaming faces

It's simple it's easy we just pray
Thank you thank you   thank you
For blessing us with this blue sky day
With all heaven's gifts shining down upon us

Oblivion

Blown to kingdom come
Is how it's expressed
By many in the military

My sudden departure burst
Scatters me abruptly about
Into bits and pieces of smithereens

My day began hurriedly
Traveling scared on a frightful
Road out of Baghdad

It ended like a breath of burnt air
Heated by an industrial blast furnace
Felt but not seen, heard or smelled

My soul is all that survived
The roadside IED surprise
My life had no time to flash before my eyes

Our Inviolable Flag

Since the stars and stripes
First waved in this brave land
Our flag has been treated badly
Without respect to say the least

Our banner's been burned and bombed
Ripped, torn and physically desecrated
By citizens, foreigners, enemies at war,
Protesters, zealots, hippies and who have you

Last time I looked our flag was still flying
Unharmed, in one piece, proudly flapping
Shining boldly in glorious red, white and blue
Looking good, looking Fourth of July fine

Do you really think you can harm our flag
I ask those who stomp, tear and burn it?
In her days she has seen worse, much worse

She can't be offended or destroyed because she still flies
We don't need laws or amendments to safeguard
Our strong, valiant, indestructible, sacred Old Glory

Pink Ribbon

The day care auditorium
Was filled to the gills
With a diverse jumble
Of preschool giggles
Getting ready to take the stage
For their annual Christmas program

How fortunate was my granddaughter
To begin her formal schooling with
Many different races and ethnic faces

My parochial education was severely limited
Colorless except for the occasional
Rosy glow on our frosty white cheeks

I asked my granddaughter to point out
Her best friend Debbie who was always
Part of our school day discussions

"She's right over there, Grandpa," Jen said.
"The one with the pink ribbon in her hair."
And there she was cute and sweet as milk chocolate

I wondered how long it would take
Before Jennie would be taught to differentiate
By skin color rather than by pink ribbons
To learn how to be more discriminating

I was certain she would not learn prejudice
From this squealing crowd of lovely diversity
And she would take what she learned to Guatemala
Where she now serves in the Peace Corps
Helping the people of Ixchiguan, San Marcos

Sailing Over The Rim

We tack westward,
Wind fitfully fills our sheets

Force four gales meet us head on,
Blast us from beneath, flip us over
Send us slowly sinking to the bottom

Wild whitecaps mark our grave
The wind's roar shouts our epitaph

Signs of Autumn

Patsy the calico
Comes in from rolling
In the garden's freshly
Turned earth and gets
Comfortable on the smooth
Surface of the cooktop range

Tiffany the gray orphan
Obtained from the vet
Scoots out from under
The drooping umbrellas of a
Long row of dying hostas
Hops on my left knee
Trading the slight chill
Of the cooling outdoors
For the warm cuddle
Of my inviting lap

The hummer whose
Wings shivered all summer
Takes a deep swig from the feeder
As it loads up to get out of town
In its usual blaze of hurry

Swinging between trees
My wife watches a leaf, bit by red,
Float like a dizzy feather
Then settle on the sway
Of her slow moving hammock

Silence

Hush
Give me a moment of quiet

If you choose to disturb
Let me hear only a whisper
As soft as the hush of hummer wings
Peace hiding in the swift motion
Of a wispy winged whirrrrrrrrrrr

Hardly heard

The Great American Novel

It's been dreamed about
By the many who have
Yet to put pen to paper

Its been started
By lots who have
Lost heart and might
Tucked drafts away in
Dusty drawers of time

Its been written
By authors who endured
The task with the spirit of inspiration
And bully strength of discipline

Born from writers famous and obscure
Whose novels are still being read
Phrases quoted, thoughts honored

When you read this you know
I wrote The Great American Novel
Condensed it and hid its soul
In the heart of these few lines

Thinking it Through

A bit of advice
For those who might
Decide to put others
Onto today's battlefields

Don't be rash
Non-prudent that is
When others' lives
Are in your hands
Slow down, think
Take your time
Think, think, think

Check back in history
See where other
Quick decisions
Have taken us

It might be a good idea
To visit a vet's hospital
And, by the way, stop
Off at a military cemetery
And muster the troops

Count the
Crosses and headstones
While you're thinking it through

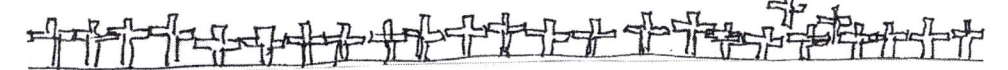

Time

You can take it
Take your time
You can give it
Give me a minute

Be with you in a second
Been waiting for hours
Passing the time of day

It marches on
Quick as a whistle
It's a wasting
Now is the time

Time and time again
From time to time
Time after time
Time out

Time heals all wounds
And we're running out of it

Walking With Dog

I include as one of my best friends
The furry lover at the end of this leash
Who accepts me and my actions
With no strings attached

His eyes always show just what
He thinks is going on in my heart
He feels the vibrations of my anxiety
Travel the length of his leash

His gait tells me to slow down
To absorb all the looks and smells
Of the beauty that may pass us by
So I absorb all I can as he takes me for a walk

Warming Warning

Warming! Warming!
Will we heed the warning?

Blistering intensity of the flame
Scorches the blazing earth
Steaming dam boils on and on and on

It starts with the glaciers
Frozen stiffs of the arctic freezer
Dripping now with frosty ice melt

Warming! Warming!
Will we heed the warning?

The chill of the blue sea
Is baked burning brown
Whale blubber touches a hot stove

Flowers and tree leaves wilt
Fiery sun kicks it up a notch
Thermometers pop their corks

Warming! Warming!
Will we heed the warning?

Our planet is an open hearth furnace
Hot breath of air is a raging forest fire
Heaving lungs are smoking embers

Warning! Warning!
We need to heed the warning of warming

Winter Rain

After a winter rain
A sundown freeze
Makes crystal chandeliers
Of massive frozen oaks

Blasts of wind
Send slivers of silver
Splashing into the evening snow
Tossing up gusts of powder

Branches clang like wind chimes
On this night of musical diamonds
Nearby a cozy child draws stars
On a window's frosty clouds

Flurries are fuming just around the corner

Writing About Nothing in Particular

I could ramble about the weather
Wet and cold wind roiling in a riot
Of swirling dizzy excitement

Or blather about the garden
Bright and bold showing off
Simmering in noon shine

Maybe buzz funny about hummers
Who act like whirling choppers
Attacking the feeder with gusto

Or stay silent like some writer
Who can't get it going
Unable to get the juices flowing

I'm a word searching poet
Who begins by writing about
Nothing, nothing in particular

Another Day

I awake and again
Wonder what it's all about?

My drive to the lake is lazy
I park on the bluff
Listen to the lake sing
Its morning song
While robust white caps
Dance the gulls awake

The day is a bad day gray
Sun is nowhere to be found
Moon, stars and satellites
Unable to open their eyes

Seems like I'm always looking
For a reasonable explanation
For all that surrounds me
Always the answers elude

But, thank God, that rare moment
Does come at unsuspecting times
Like now when I seem to know
Without really knowing a thing

Like knowing the sun, moon and stars
Are still brilliant behind those dark clouds
And the lake will soon be quiet and calm

Pentecost

We drift, dead in the water and hope
To seize a stiff breeze to sail on our way

We feel helpless but believe, during
This uncertain calm, harried by anxiety and doubt,
Its force still simmers somewhere

It comes softly and builds to a force suddenly
Its power fills our sails and soon billows
Our spinnaker pulling us towards home

Here's to faith, I graciously pray, as we hear
Our sheets flap wildly in the wind

Skyrockets

Watching a July shower of sparkling confetti fall
Flame coloring the cotton candy clouds
We think of our freedom fighters whose spirits lit the fuse

When the band plays *Stars and Stripes Forever*
Invigorating every patriotic heart
We again see those gallant fighters marching in glorious step

Our proud nation again struts its stuff
Celebrating this monumental fourth day of July
Our nation's history is marked by explosions in the sky

Morning Chorus

A gaggle of geese
Harmonize on the horizon
Nightingales trill in the trees

It's a melodic dawn
On a mute lake
Of silent silver ripples

A graceful white bird
Who rarely toots its horn
Sings a swan song solo